CHICAGO
Bulls

BY ELLEN LABRECQUE

Published by The Child's World®
1980 Lookout Drive • Mankato, MN 56003-1705
800-599-READ • www.childsworld.com

Acknowledgments
The Child's World®: Mary Berendes, Publishing Director
Red Line Editorial: Editorial direction
The Design Lab: Design
Amnet: Production

Design elements: PhotoDisc, Viorika Prikhodko/iStockphoto

Photographs ©: Jeffrey Phelps/AP Images, cover, title;
Charles Rex Arbogast/AP Images, 5; John Raoux/AP
Images, 6; Dale Pickoff/AP Images, 9; Paul Sancya/AP
Images, 10; Martha Irvine/AP Images, 13; AP Images,
17; Chuck Burton/AP Images, 18; Evan Vucci/AP Images,
21; Kirthmon Dozier/AP Images, 22; Nam Y. Huh/AP
Images, 25, 26

ISBN 978-1623234973
LCCN 2013931360

Printed in the United States of America
Mankato, MN
July, 2014
PA02237

About the Author

Ellen Labrecque has written books for young readers on basketball, tennis, ice hockey, and other sports. Ellen used to work for *Sports Illustrated Kids* magazine and has written about many NBA stars. She likes to watch basketball. The Philadelphia 76ers are her favorite team.

Table of Contents

Go, Bulls!

Holy cow! Or should we say *Holy Bulls!* The Chicago Bulls are an awesome basketball team. One of the greatest basketball players of all time played for the Bulls. This team has fans all over the Midwest. Are you one of those fans? Let's meet the Chicago Bulls! Go, Bulls!

Derrick Rose and the Chicago Bulls are always tough to beat.

Who Are the Bulls?

The Chicago Bulls play in the National Basketball Association (NBA). They are one of 30 teams in the NBA. The NBA includes the Eastern Conference and the Western Conference. The Bulls play in the Central Division of the Eastern Conference. The Eastern Conference champion plays the Western Conference champion in the **NBA Finals**. The Bulls have won the NBA title six times!

Chicago Bulls star Luol Deng was born in the African nation of Sudan.

Where They Came From

The Bulls joined the NBA in 1966. They weren't the first pro basketball team to play in Chicago. The Chicago Bruins played in the American Basketball League from 1925 to 1931. Two other Chicago teams played in the NBA before the Bulls. They were the Chicago Stags (1949–50) and the Chicago Packers/Zephyrs (1961–63). Chicago finally got an NBA team to stick around when the Bulls came to town!

The Bulls' Jerry Sloan goes up for a rebound in a 1968 game against the New York Knicks.

Who They Play

The Bulls play 82 games each season. That's a lot of basketball! They play every other NBA team at least once each season. They play teams in their division and conference more often. The Detroit Pistons are one of the Bulls' biggest **rivals**. The two teams play in the same division. Both have a history of playing tough **defense**. They have met in the **playoffs** six times through 2012. The last time was in the 2007 Eastern Conference **semifinals**. The Pistons won the series, 4–2.

Games between the Bulls and Pistons are always tough battles.

Where They Play

The Bulls used to play their games in Chicago Stadium. In 1994, they moved across the street to the United Center. This large arena seats 20,917 fans for Bulls games. A bronze statue stands outside the United Center. The statue is of Michael Jordan. Jordan led the Bulls to six NBA titles. Three of the titles were won in the Chicago Stadium era. The other three were won after the Bulls moved to the United Center.

The Michael Jordan statue welcomes fans to the United Center.

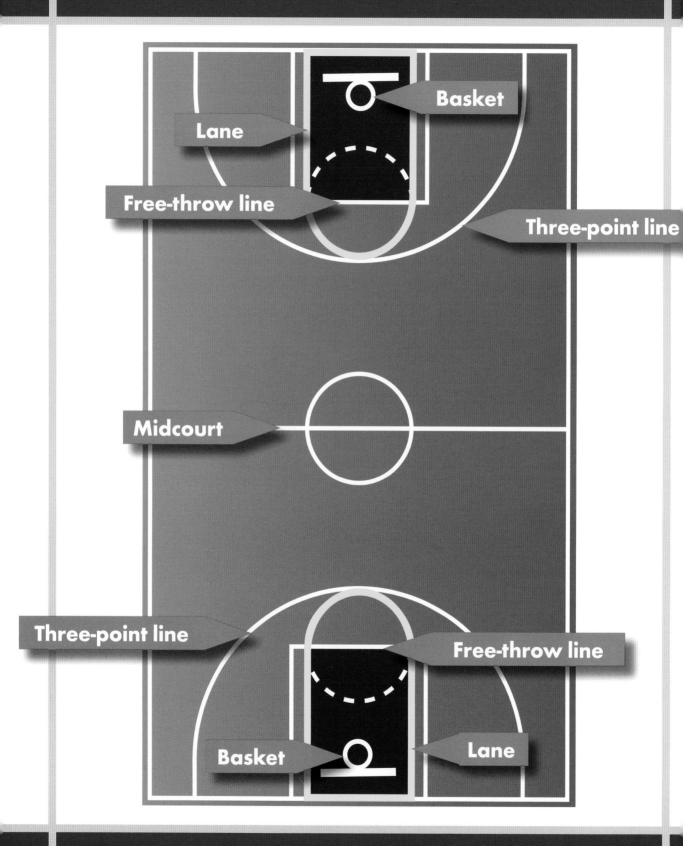

Basket

Lane

Free-throw line

Three-point line

Midcourt

Three-point line

Free-throw line

Basket

Lane

The Basketball Court

Basketball is played on a court made of wood. An NBA court is 94 feet (29 m) long. A painted line shows the middle of the court. Other lines lay out the free-throw area. The space below each basket is known as the "lane." The baskets at each end are 10 feet (3 m) high. The metal rims of the baskets stick out over the court. Nylon nets hang from the rims.

Big Days

The Chicago Bulls have had many great moments, especially in the 1990s. Here are three of the greatest:

1991: Michael Jordan led the Bulls to their first NBA championship.

1993: Chicago became the first NBA team in 27 seasons to win three championships in a row. Jordan was named NBA Finals Most Valuable Player (MVP) for the third straight season.

1998: The Bulls won their third straight title . . . again! Jordan led the NBA in scoring for the tenth time!

Bulls star Michael Jordan (left) and coach Phil Jackson (right) won six NBA titles together.

Tough Days

The Bulls can't win all their games. Some games or seasons don't turn out well. The players keep trying to play their best, though. Here are some of the toughest seasons in Bulls history:

1976: The Bulls won only 24 games and lost 58. It was their worst record until 1998–99, after Michael Jordan left.

2001: Chicago won only 15 games. There was a good reason. The Bulls had the youngest team in NBA history. Most of the players were 22 years old or younger.

2004: The Bulls missed the playoffs for the sixth straight season. Bulls fans didn't lose hope! The team made the playoffs in 2005.

Not much went right for the "Baby Bulls" in 2001.

Meet the Fans

Did you know that President Barack Obama is a Bulls fan? He lived and worked in Chicago for many years. President Obama will be the first to tell you that Chicago is one cold city during the winter! That is why indoor basketball is the perfect sport for this city. Bulls fans can stay warm while cheering for their team.

President Barack Obama watches his favorite team, the Bulls!

Heroes Then . . .

Many believe **guard** Michael Jordan was the best
NBA player of all time. Jordan could do it all.
He could score lots of points and play defense. He
could also leap high into the air for **slam dunks**.
Forward Scottie Pippen was Jordan's sidekick
throughout the 1990s. He was also a star in his own
right. Star forward Bob Love played for the Bulls
in the 1960s and 1970s. Love could shoot very well
with either hand. Jerry Sloan also played around this
time. He played great defense. Later, he won more
than 1,000 games as coach for the Utah Jazz.

Many tried, but few could defend against Michael Jordan.

Heroes Now . . .

The Bulls had the first pick in the 2008 **NBA Draft**. They selected **point guard** Derrick Rose. He leads the Bulls' **offense** with his passing and drives to the basket. He's one of the best young passers the NBA has ever seen. Rose was named the NBA MVP in 2011. **Center** Joakim Noah is a defensive force. He is scrappy under the basket and gets lots of **blocks** and **rebounds**. Together, these players have helped the Bulls rise back to the top of the NBA.

Derrick Rose has run the Bulls' offense since 2008.

Jersey

Shorts

Knee brace

Socks

Basketball shoes

Gearing Up

Chicago Bulls players wear the team's uniform and special basketball sneakers. Some wear other pads to protect themselves. Check out this picture of Joakim Noah and learn about what NBA players wear.

THE BASKETBALL

NBA basketballs are made of leather. Several pieces are held together with rubber edges. Inside the leather ball is a hollow ball of rubber. This is filled with air. The leather is covered with little bumps called "pebbles." The pebbles help players get a good grip on the ball. The basketball used in the Women's National Basketball Association (WNBA) is slightly smaller than the men's basketball.

Bulls center Joakim Noah is one of the NBA's best defenders.

Note: All numbers shown are through the 2012–13 season.

HIGH SCORERS

These players have scored the most points for the Bulls.

PLAYER	POINTS
Michael Jordan	29,277
Scottie Pippen	15,123

HELPING HAND

Here are Chicago's all-time leaders in **assists**.

PLAYER	ASSISTS
Michael Jordan	5,012
Scottie Pippen	4,494

CLEANING THE BOARDS

Rebounds are a big part of the game. Here are the Bulls' best rebounders.

PLAYER	REBOUNDS
Michael Jordan	5,836
Tom Boerwinkle	5,745

MOST THREE-POINT SHOTS MADE

Shots taken from behind a line about 23 feet (7 m) from the basket are worth three points. Here are the Bulls' best at these long-distance shots.

PLAYER	THREE-POINT BASKETS
Kirk Hinrich	883
Ben Gordon	770

COACH

Who coached the Bulls to the most wins?

Phil Jackson, 545

assists passes to teammates that lead directly to making baskets

blocks when a defender stops a shot before it reaches the basket

center a player (usually the tallest on the team) who plays close to the basket

defense when a team doesn't have the ball and is trying to keep the other team from scoring

forward one of two tall players who rebound and score near the basket

guard one of two players who set up plays, pass to teammates closer to the basket, and shoot from farther away

NBA Draft a meeting of all the NBA teams at which they choose college players to join them

NBA Finals the seven-game NBA championship series, in which the champion must win four games

offense when a team has the ball and is trying to score

playoffs a series of games between 16 teams that decides which two teams will play in the NBA Finals

point guard the team's main ball handler, who brings the ball up the court and sets up the offense

rebounds missed shots that bounce off the backboard or rim and are grabbed by another player

rivals teams that play each other often and have an ongoing competition

semifinals the next-to-last round of the playoffs, with the winners going on to play in the final series

slam dunk a shot in which a player stuffs the ball down into the basket

BOOKS

Frisch, Aaron. *Chicago Bulls*. Mankato, MN: Creative Paperbacks, 2012.

Hareas, John. *Championship Teams*. New York: Scholastic, 2010.

Smallwood, John N. *Megastars*. New York: Scholastic, 2011.

Woog, Adam. *Derrick Rose*. Detroit: Lucent Books, 2010.

WEB SITES

Visit our Web page for links about the Chicago Bulls and other NBA teams: **childsworld.com/links**

Note to Parents, Teachers, and Librarians: We routinely verify our Web links to make sure they are safe and active sites. So encourage your readers to check them out!

INDEX